GREAT MINDS® WIT & WISDOM

Grade 2 Module 4
Good Eating

Student Edition

GREAT MINDS

Great Minds® is the creator of *Eureka Math*®,
Wit & Wisdom®, *Alexandria Plan*™, and *PhD Science*®.

Published by Great Minds PBC
greatminds.org

© 2023 Great Minds PBC. All rights reserved. No part of this work may be reproduced or used in any form or by any means—graphic, electronic, or mechanical, including photocopying or information storage and retrieval systems—without written permission from the copyright holder.

Printed in the USA

A-Print

1 2 3 4 5 6 7 8 9 10 QDG 27 26 25 24 23

979-8-88588-732-8

STUDENT EDITION

Handout 1A: Digestive System

Handout 2A: Fluency Homework

Handout 4A: Evidence Organizer

Handout 5A: Digestive System

Handout 5B: Digestive System Response Cards

Handout 5C: Vocabulary Graphic Organizer

Handout 7A: Informative Writing Checklist

Handout 9A: Suffixes –*ful* and -*less*

Handout 10A: Fluency Homework

Handout 10B: Reflexive Pronouns

Handout 11A: Word Relationships

Handout 12A: Experimentation with Reflexive Pronouns

Handout 13A: Academic Vocabulary: *Cooperation*

Handout 14A: Focusing Question Task 2 Evidence Organizer

Handout 15A: Opinion Writing Checklist

Handout 15B: Frayer Model

Handout 16A: Socratic Seminar Self-Reflection

Handout 16B: Possessive Nouns

Handout 17A: Fluency Homework

Handout 17B: Singular and Plural Possessive Nouns

Handout 18A: Experimentation with Possessive Nouns

Handout 19A: Word Riddles

Handout 19B: Steps in a Process Evidence Organizer

Handout 19C: Experimentation with Commas in Letters

Handout 20A: Commas in Letters

Handout 22A: Fluency Homework

Handout 22B: Nutrient Word Riddles

Handout 23A: Vocabulary Graphic Organizer for *energy*

Handout 24A: Evidence Organizer

Handout 27A: Opinion Writing Checklist

Handout 27B: "Can Milk Make You Happy?"

Handout 27C: Author's Point and Reasons

Handout 28A: Word Parts

Handout 29A: End-of-Module Task Evidence Organizer

Handout 32A: Opinion Writing Checklist
Handout 32B: Socratic Seminar Self-Reflection
Volume of Reading Reflection Questions
Wit & Wisdom Family Tip Sheet

Name:

Handout 1A: Digestive System

Directions: Fill in the boxes as you learn more about the digestive system in Module 4.

Digestive System	
Definition: Parts of the body that work together to break down food.	**Facts/Characteristics:**
Picture:	**Vocabulary:**

Name: _____

Handout 2A: Fluency Homework

Directions: Choose one of the text options to read aloud.

Option A

> Human beings need food in order to feed the body. The healthier the food is, the better it is for your body. But what happens to food once we chew and swallow? Food is processed in the body by the digestive system. It is broken down into smaller and smaller pieces. Then it is absorbed into the body. This gives the body fuel to produce energy.
>
> 66 words
>
> Prior, Jennifer. *The Digestive System*. Teacher Created Materials.

Student Performance Checklist:	Day 1 You	Day 1 Listener*	Day 2 You	Day 2 Listener*	Day 3 You	Day 3 Listener*	Day 4 You	Day 4 Listener*
Read the passage three to five times.								
Read with appropriate phrasing and pausing.								
Read with appropriate expression.								
Read at a good pace, not too fast and not too slow.								
Read to be heard and understood.								

*Adult or peer

Name:

Option B

> How do you keep your digestive tract in top shape? Eat well, drink water when you are thirsty, and get regular exercise. If you do these things, the good things will get into your system and the unwanted waste will move out quickly. You'll feel well. You'll have all the energy you need.
>
> 53 words
>
> Taylor-Butler, Christine. *The Digestive System*. Scholastic Inc. 2008.

Student Performance Checklist:	Day 1 You	Day 1 Listener*	Day 2 You	Day 2 Listener*	Day 3 You	Day 3 Listener*	Day 4 You	Day 4 Listener*
Read the passage three to five times.								
Read with appropriate phrasing and pausing.								
Read with appropriate expression.								
Read at a good pace, not too fast and not too slow.								
Read to be heard and understood.								

*Adult or peer

Name:

Handout 4A: Evidence Organizer

Directions: Use this Evidence Organizer to plan for Focusing Question Task 1.

Choose One (circle):	
stomach	small Intestine
Research Question: What important jobs does this organ do as part of the digestive system?	
1	
2	
Conclusion: Why is this part of the system important?	

Name:

Handout 5A: Digestive System

Directions: Read along with your teacher about the digestive system. Place your Response Cards on the diagram below to label the parts. Do NOT glue or tape them down.

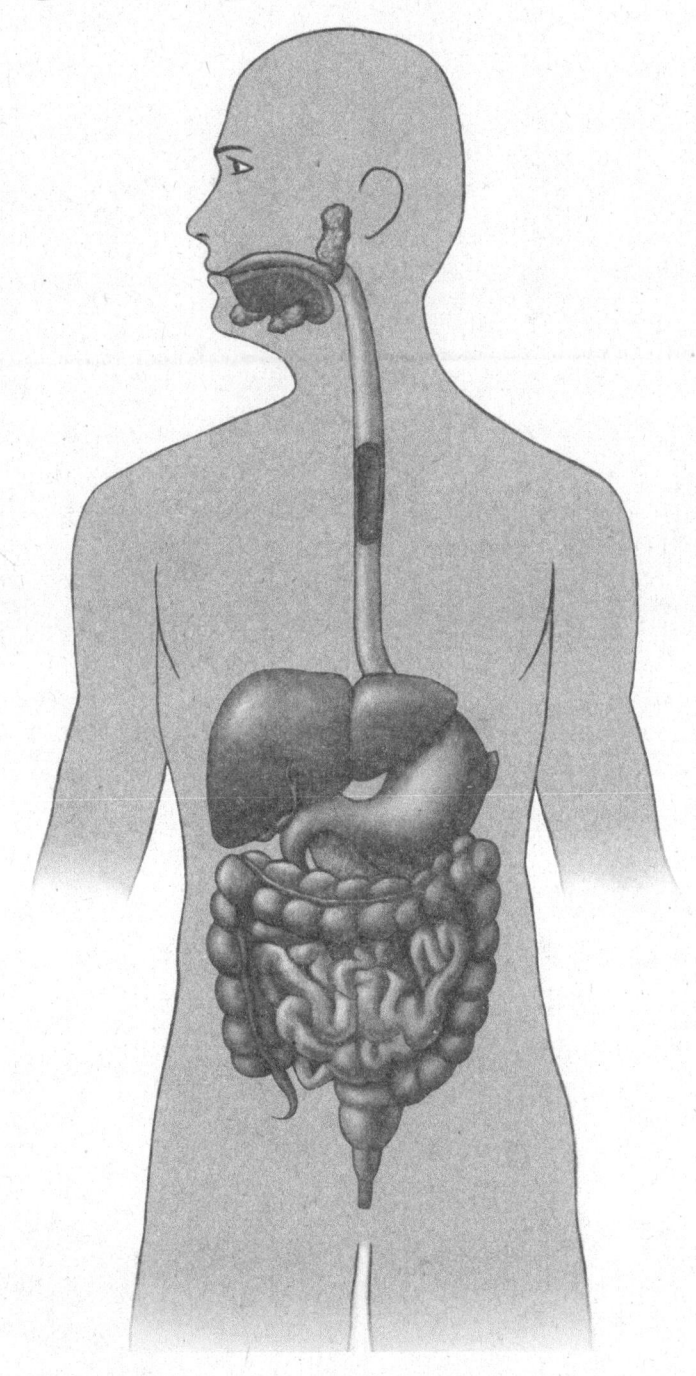

Name: _____

Handout 5B:
Digestive System Response Cards

Directions: Cut out the six cards below.

mouth	esophagus
stomach	small intestine
large intestine	rectum

Name: _____

Handout 5C:
Vocabulary Graphic Organizer

Directions: Complete the handout about the word absorb.

absorb

1. **Definition:** To take in through very small openings.	2. **Sentence(s):**
3. **Examples:**	4. **Non-examples:**
5. **Synonyms:**	6. **Antonyms:**

Name:

Handout 7A:
Informative Writing Checklist

Directions: After completing your paragraph, circle ☺ Yes or ☹ Not Yet to answer each prompt. Be sure to include a writing goal.

Reading Comprehension	Self	Peer	Teacher
I understand the digestion process that takes place in either the stomach or small intestine.	☺ ☹ Yes Not Yet	☺ ☹ Yes Not Yet	☺ ☹ Yes Not Yet
Structure	**Self**	**Peer**	**Teacher**
I start the paragraph with an introduction.	☺ ☹ Yes Not Yet	☺ ☹ Yes Not Yet	☺ ☹ Yes Not Yet
I include a topic statement.	☺ ☹ Yes Not Yet	☺ ☹ Yes Not Yet	☺ ☹ Yes Not Yet
I include at least two points with evidence.	☺ ☹ Yes Not Yet	☺ ☹ Yes Not Yet	☺ ☹ Yes Not Yet

	Self	Peer	Teacher
I end the paragraph with a conclusion.	☺ ☺ Yes Not Yet	☺ ☺ Yes Not Yet	☺ ☺ Yes Not Yet
Style	Self	Peer	Teacher
I use topic-specific words.	☺ ☺ Yes Not Yet	☺ ☺ Yes Not Yet	☺ ☺ Yes Not Yet
Conventions	Self	Peer	Teacher
I use contractions correctly.	☺ ☺ Yes Not Yet	☺ ☺ Yes Not Yet	☺ ☺ Yes Not Yet
I use my best spelling. A B C	☺ ☺ Yes Not Yet	☺ ☺ Yes Not Yet	☺ ☺ Yes Not Yet
I use end punctuation. . ? !	☺ ☺ Yes Not Yet	☺ ☺ Yes Not Yet	☺ ☺ Yes Not Yet
I write complete sentences that have subjects and verbs.	☺ ☺ Yes Not Yet	☺ ☺ Yes Not Yet	☺ ☺ Yes Not Yet
Total number of ☺ :			

Name:

My writing goal is

___

___

___

Teacher Feedback

Name:

Handout 9A: Suffixes –*ful* and –*less*

Directions: Cut out the word cards and sort them into three categories.

joy	joyful	careful
harmful	harm	thank
care	thankless	careless
joyless	harmless	fearless
fearful	fear	hopeless
hopeful	hope	power
powerless	powerful	colorless
colorful	color	thankful

Name:

Handout 10A: Fluency Homework

<u>Directions:</u> Choose one of the text options to read aloud.

Option A

> The beggar counted the buttons. There were five. "Oy, if only I had one more button," he said. The shamas said nothing. "Oy, if only I had one more button!" Still the shamas was silent. "OY, IF ONLY I HAD ONE MORE BUTTON!" Finally the shamas spoke. "Look, mister, I won't give you a button. Nobody in this town will give you a button." "Why not?" asked the beggar. "Because we're poor, Mr. Beggar. We don't give to each other any more."
>
> 82 words
>
> Davis, Aubrey. *Bone Button Borscht*. Kids Can Press, 1995.

Student Performance Checklist:	Day 1		Day 2		Day 3		Day 4	
	You	Listener*	You	Listener*	You	Listener*	You	Listener*
Read the passage three to five times.								
Read with appropriate phrasing and pausing.								
Read with appropriate expression.								
Read at a good pace, not too fast and not too slow.								
Read to be heard and understood.								

*Adult or peer

Name:

Option B

> The years passed. One by one the beggar's bone buttons were lost. But it is a strange thing, a wonder, perhaps. The townsfolk learned they didn't really need the buttons. They learned to make borscht without them. And they learned to help one another without borscht, even in hard times. That was the real miracle the beggar left behind.
>
> 53 words
>
> Davis, Aubrey. *Bone Button Borscht*. Kids Can Press, 1995.

Student Performance Checklist:	Day 1 You	Day 1 Listener*	Day 2 You	Day 2 Listener*	Day 3 You	Day 3 Listener*	Day 4 You	Day 4 Listener*
Read the passage three to five times.			▓	▓	▓	▓		
Read with appropriate phrasing and pausing.	▓	▓			▓	▓		
Read with appropriate expression.	▓	▓	▓	▓				
Read at a good pace, not too fast and not too slow.	▓	▓	▓	▓	▓	▓		
Read to be heard and understood.	▓	▓	▓	▓	▓	▓		

*Adult or peer

Name: _____

Handout 10B: Reflexive Pronouns

Directions: Circle the reflexive pronoun. Draw an arrow from the reflexive pronoun to the noun or pronoun it reflects. Then, answer the question below the sentences.

Example: "Where's the town?" the beggar asked (himself.)

1. The people crammed themselves inside.

2. He warmed himself by the stove.

3. Leah thought to herself before giving the beggar a spoon.

4. "You can help yourselves to borscht."

5. "Please don't go, why are you leaving by yourself?"

6. The shamas wondered to himself who the beggar was.

What would happen to the sentences above if they did not have reflexive pronouns?

_____

_____

_____

_____

Name: _____

Handout 11A: Word Relationships

Directions:

1. Read the sentence.
2. Act out the meaning of the underlined word.
3. Think of an example of the word in real life.

"One dark winter's night a ragged little beggar <u>hobbled</u> along a lonely road."

Real-life example: A person might <u>hobble</u> if or when _____

_____

"Here come three soldiers. Soldiers are always hungry. But we have little enough for ourselves." And they <u>hurried</u> to hide their food.

Real-life example: _____

_____

"Wait!" called the beggar, "I'll need bowls and cups, and a knife and a ladle and a spoon. Oh, and a pot, maybe?" The shamas <u>sped</u> down the road to the tailor's door and knocked.

Real-life example: A person might <u>speed</u> somewhere if _____

_____

"Thank God for synagogues!" he cried and <u>rushed</u> inside.

Real-life example: _____

_____

Name: _____

Handout 12A: Experimentation with Reflexive Pronouns

Directions: Write the correct reflexive pronoun in each of the sentences below. Circle the reflexive pronoun and draw an arrow from it to the word it reflects.

Use the following chart as a tool.

Personal Pronoun	Reflexive Pronoun
I	myself
you	yourself
he	himself
she	herself
it	itself
we	ourselves
you (plural)	yourselves
they	themselves

1. The soldiers could not make the soup by _____.

2. "I'm so hungry," the beggar thought to _____.

3. They walked down the road by _____.

4. We do not have enough food to feed _____!

5. "I do not have food for _____," said the woman.

6. He trudged down the road feeling sorry for _____.

Stop and Jot: How do you choose the correct reflexive pronoun?

_____

_____

_____

Name:

Handout 13A:
Academic Vocabulary: *Cooperation*

Directions: Complete the handout about the word *cooperation*.

cooperation (noun): the act of working together

	Examples	Non-Examples
Real-Life		
Text		

Name:

Handout 14A: Focusing Question Task 2 Evidence Organizer

Directions: After you form your opinion, use this planner to record the evidence you need to write your answer for Focusing Question Task 2. Then, look at your evidence to decide a reason.

Question: Who benefited the most from making the soup in *Bone Button Borscht*?	
(circle one) Townspeople OR Beggar	
Reason	

Name:

Handout 15A:
Opinion Writing Checklist

Directions: Circle ☺ Yes or ☹ Not Yet to answer each prompt. Then, set a writing goal.

Comprehension	Self	Peer	Teacher
I understand how the beggar and the townspeople benefitted from each other.	☺ ☹ Yes Not Yet	☺ ☹ Yes Not Yet	☺ ☹ Yes Not Yet
Structure	**Self**	**Peer**	**Teacher**
I respond to all parts of the prompt.	☺ ☹ Yes Not Yet	☺ ☹ Yes Not Yet	☺ ☹ Yes Not Yet
I introduce the topic I am writing about.	☺ ☹ Yes Not Yet	☺ ☹ Yes Not Yet	☺ ☹ Yes Not Yet
I write an opinion statement.	☺ ☹ Yes Not Yet	☺ ☹ Yes Not Yet	☺ ☹ Yes Not Yet

I write two or more reasons to support my opinion statement.	🙂 😐 Yes Not Yet	🙂 😐 Yes Not Yet	🙂 😐 Yes Not Yet
I write a conclusion that restates or repeats the opinion.	🙂 😐 Yes Not Yet	🙂 😐 Yes Not Yet	🙂 😐 Yes Not Yet
Conventions			
I use my best spelling. **A B C**	🙂 😐 Yes Not Yet	🙂 😐 Yes Not Yet	🙂 😐 Yes Not Yet
I use end punctuation. **. ? !**	🙂 😐 Yes Not Yet	🙂 😐 Yes Not Yet	🙂 😐 Yes Not Yet
I write complete sentences that have subjects and verbs.	🙂 😐 Yes Not Yet	🙂 😐 Yes Not Yet	🙂 😐 Yes Not Yet
Total number of 🙂 :			

Name:

My writing goal is

Teacher Feedback

Name:

Handout 15B: Frayer Model

Directions: Complete the Frayer Model for *banquet*.

Definition:	Facts/Characteristics:
Examples:	Nonexamples:

Word:

banquet

Name:

Handout 16A:
Socratic Seminar Self-Reflection

Directions: Use one of the letters below to describe how often you performed each action during the Socratic Seminar.

A = I always did that.

S = I sometimes did that.

N = I'll do that next time.

Expectation	Evaluation (A, S, N)
I spoke on topic.	
I listened to appreciate.	
I looked at the speaker.	
I recounted details for *Bone Button Borscht* based on our Read Alouds.	

Expectation	Evaluation (A, S, N)
I spoke only when no one else was speaking.	
I used kind words.	
I varied inflection when speaking.	

Name: _____

Handout 16B: Possessive Nouns

Part 1 Directions: Circle the possessive phrase in each sentence. Then, use the "of" test to explain each possessive phrase.

1. The second soldier slept in the baker's house.

   The baker's house = The _____ of the _____ .

2. The beggar's buttons were lost.

   The beggar's buttons = The _____ of the _____ .

3. The soldiers' feet were tired from trudging down the road.

   The soldiers' feet = The _____ of the _____ .

4. The peasants' eyes grew round as they watched the soldiers drop the stones into the pot.

   The peasants' eyes = The _____ of the _____ .

Part 2 Directions: Circle the word with the apostrophe in each sentence. Use the "of" test to determine whether the word is a possessive noun. If the word is a contraction, draw a line through the sentence.

1) The fire's heat. The _____ of the _____.

2) The peasants' meal. The _____ of the _____.

3) "We're hungry!" said the beggars. The _____ of the _____.

Why do writers use apostrophes in possessive phrases?

_____

_____

_____

_____

Name:

Handout 17A: Fluency Homework

Directions: Read aloud the text below. Have an adult or peer initial the unshaded boxes each day that you read the passage.

> Look at all the vegetables! Vegetables are the parts of plants that are grown to be eaten. Most are annuals. Some are perennials. It is good for us to eat vegetables. They are nutritious and help keep our bodies strong and healthy. They are tasty, too.
>
> 40 words
>
> Gibbons, Gail. *The Vegetables We Eat*. 2007. Holiday House, 2015.

G2 > M4 > Handout 17A • WIT & WISDOM®

Student Performance Checklist:	Day 1 You	Day 1 Listener*	Day 2 You	Day 2 Listener*	Day 3 You	Day 3 Listener*	Day 4 You	Day 4 Listener*
Read the passage three to five times.								
Read with appropriate phrasing and pausing.								
Read with appropriate expression.								
Read at a good pace, not too fast and not too slow.								
Read to be heard and understood.								

*Adult or peer

Name: _____

Handout 17B: Singular and Plural Possessive Nouns

Directions:

1. Circle the possessive nouns in the sentences below.

2. Use the location of the apostrophe and the meaning in the sentence to help you determine whether the noun is singular or plural. Label each noun with an <u>S</u> for "singular" and <u>P</u> for "plural."

   1) This beet's color is red. ____

   2) The beans' pods can be eaten. ____

   3) The corn's husk is green. ____

   4) We eat some plants' seeds. ____

Why is the location of the apostrophe important in possessive nouns?

_____

_____

_____

_____

Name:

Handout 18A: Experimentation with Possessive Nouns

Directions: Rewrite the underlined parts of the sentences to include a possessive.

Sentence	Rewrite with Possessive
Example: We eat the <u>leaves of these vegetables</u>.	We eat the <u>vegetables' leaves</u>.
The <u>buds of a cauliflower</u> are eaten.	The _____ are eaten.
The <u>bulbs of onions</u> are eaten.	The _____ are eaten.
The <u>stems of these vegetables</u> are eaten.	These _____ are eaten.
The <u>color of the pumpkin</u> is orange.	The _____ is orange.
We can eat the <u>seeds of a lima bean</u>.	We can eat _____ .

Name:

Handout 19A: Word Riddles

Directions: Cut the cards apart to play a matching game. Then, sort the cards into piles that fit together.

I am a perennial.	a plant that grows for many seasons without having to be replanted.
I am an annual.	a plant that grows for only one season.
I am a botanist.	a scientist who studies plants.
I am a carrot, a root vegetable.	long and thin, growing beneath the ground. Pull me up by my leaves and stem and there I'll be found.

Name:

Directions: Cut the cards apart to play a matching game. Then, sort the cards into piles that fit together.

I am a potato, a tuber vegetable.	At the end of a root, that's where I am found. I can be little or big and almost round. I come in colors red, yellow, purple or brown!
I am a bean, a seed vegetable.	You know me by one name, but I have another. My pods are long and lean and usually green.
I am a shovel.	In your home garden, I am just the right size to turn your soil and get you started.
I am a plow.	On the farm, it takes a big machine like me to ready the soil for the seeds.

Name: _____

Directions: Cut the cards apart to play a matching game. Then, sort the cards into piles that fit together.

I am fertilizer.	You use me on the farm and in your garden to help give the soil nutrients, or food, to give to your plants.
I am a trowel.	I am used in a home garden to dig holes to plant the starter plants or seedlings.
I am a harrow.	On the big farm, I smooth the soil before the planter places the seeds in the ground.
harvested	The vegetables are ready to be picked or _____ at the end of the growing season on the farm and in the garden.

Name: _____

Handout 19B: Steps in a Process Evidence Organizer

Directions: Use this chart to record the steps in a process and the details.

Text: *The Vegetables We Eat*		
Process: Steps in planting a big vegetable farm.		
	Step	Details
Step 1		
Step 2		
Step 3		
Step 4		

Name:

Handout 19C: Experimentation with Commas in Letters

Directions: Add commas to the letter below. The letter is from a reader to Gail Gibbons.

May 6 2017

Dear Ms. Gibbons

Thank you for teaching me about the different kinds of vegetables we eat. I never knew that there were eight different categories of vegetables.

Sincerely

Edgar

Directions: Write a letter thanking someone for the food you eat. Remember to use commas in the correct places.

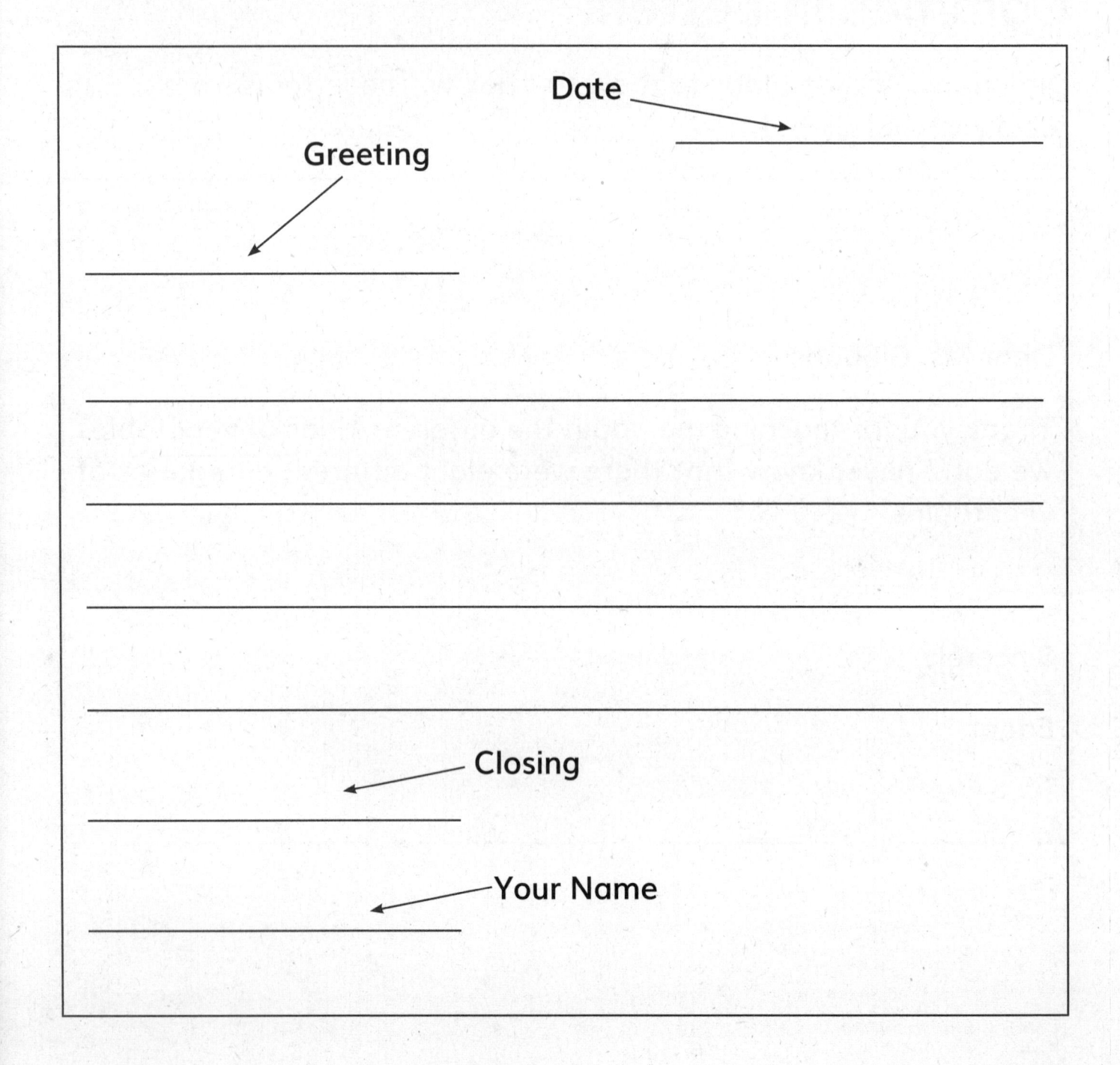

Date →

Greeting ↓

Closing ←

Your Name ←

Name:

Handout 20A: Commas in Letters

Directions: Use the template to write a letter using commas in the correct places. Circle your commas when you finish your letter.

Name:

Handout 22A: Fluency Homework

Directions: Choose one of the text options to read aloud. Have an adult or peer initial the unshaded boxes each day that you read the passage.

Option A

> Hunger sends you strong signals. It lets you know that eating is the most important thing you do each day. The food you eat and drink keeps you alive. It builds, protects, and energizes your body.
>
> 36 words
>
> Rockwell, Lizzy. *Good Enough to Eat: A Kid's Guide to Food and Nutrition.* HarperCollins, 1999.

Student Performance Checklist:	Day 1		Day 2		Day 3		Day 4	
	You	Listener*	You	Listener*	You	Listener*	You	Listener*
Read the passage three to five times.								
Read with appropriate phrasing and pausing.								
Read with appropriate expression.								
Read at a good pace, not too fast and not too slow.								
Read to be heard and understood.								

*Adult or peer

Name:

Option B

> Every food contains at least one nutrient, but healthy foods have lots of them. Your body uses different nutrients in different ways. Digestion is the way food is broken down so that nutrients can be absorbed into your body.
>
> 39 words
>
> Rockwell, Lizzy. *Good Enough to Eat: A Kid's Guide to Food and Nutrition.* HarperCollins, 1999.

Student Performance Checklist:	Day 1 You	Day 1 Listener*	Day 2 You	Day 2 Listener*	Day 3 You	Day 3 Listener*	Day 4 You	Day 4 Listener*
Read the passage three to five times.								
Read with appropriate phrasing and pausing.								
Read with appropriate expression.								
Read at a good pace, not too fast and not too slow.								
Read to be heard and understood.								

*Adult or peer

Handout 22B: Nutrient Word Riddles

Directions: Complete the Sentence Frame. Answer the questions below using the word bank and your text as a reference.

Nutrients are the parts of _____ that the body needs to

do its _____ .

carbohydrates	*fats*	*protein*
water	*vitamins*	*minerals*

There are lots of me in butter and cream, but don't put too much of me in your bloodstream.	
I'm made of specks of metal and rock. If you don't have me, you'll need to go to the doc!	
Most of your body is made of me. I clean and cool you, and make you go pee!	
I am found in milk, meat, eggs, and cheese. I make you strong, so eat me, please!	
Starchy foods love me, and so do you. I give you lots of energy, so please start to chew!	
A, B, C, D, my names have lots of letters. C helps you heal, and A helps you see better!	

Name: _____

Handout 23A: Vocabulary Graphic Organizer for *energy*

Directions: Complete the graphic organizer about the word *energy*.

energy

1. **Definition:** The power or ability to do work. Picture:	2. **Sentence(s):**
3. **Examples:**	4. **Non-examples:**
5. **Synonyms:**	6. **Antonyms:**

Name:

Handout 24A: Evidence Organizer

Directions: Use this Evidence Organizer to record evidence to help you choose a nutritious food.

Food	Reason	Evidence
strawberry		
orange		
carrot		
broccoli		

Name:

Handout 27A: Opinion Writing Checklist

Directions: Circle ☺ Yes or ☹ Not Yet to answer each prompt. Then, set a writing goal.

Comprehension	Self	Peer	Teacher
I understand how to make good choices about food.	☺ ☹ Yes Not Yet	☺ ☹ Yes Not Yet	☺ ☹ Yes Not Yet
Structure	**Self**	**Peer**	**Teacher**
I respond to all parts of the prompt.	☺ ☹ Yes Not Yet	☺ ☹ Yes Not Yet	☺ ☹ Yes Not Yet
I introduce the topic I am writing about.	☺ ☹ Yes Not Yet	☺ ☹ Yes Not Yet	☺ ☹ Yes Not Yet
I write an opinion statement.	☺ ☹ Yes Not Yet	☺ ☹ Yes Not Yet	☺ ☹ Yes Not Yet

I write two or more reasons to support my opinion statement.	🙂 😐 Yes Not Yet	🙂 😐 Yes Not Yet	🙂 😐 Yes Not Yet
I write one or more pieces of evidence about the reasons.	🙂 😐 Yes Not Yet	🙂 😐 Yes Not Yet	🙂 😐 Yes Not Yet
I write a conclusion that restates or repeats the opinion.	🙂 😐 Yes Not Yet	🙂 😐 Yes Not Yet	🙂 😐 Yes Not Yet
Development			
I use linking works to make connections between sentences.	🙂 😐 Yes Not Yet	🙂 😐 Yes Not Yet	🙂 😐 Yes Not Yet
Conventions			
I use my best spelling. A B C	🙂 😐 Yes Not Yet	🙂 😐 Yes Not Yet	🙂 😐 Yes Not Yet

Name:

I use end punctuation. . ? !	🙂 😐 Yes Not Yet	🙂 😐 Yes Not Yet	🙂 😐 Yes Not Yet
I write complete sentences that have subjects and verbs.	🙂 😐 Yes Not Yet	🙂 😐 Yes Not Yet	🙂 😐 Yes Not Yet
Total number of 🙂 :			

My writing goal is _____

_____

_____

Teacher Feedback

Name:

Handout 27B: "Can Milk Make You Happy?"

<u>Directions:</u> Listen and follow along as the text is read aloud. Then, complete Handout 27C with the author's point and reasons.

"Can Milk Make You Happy?"
Adapted from an article by Faith Hickman Brynie

We know that a diet full of whole grains, fruits, and vegetables is healthy. It might even help us avoid some diseases such as cancer or heart disease. But did you know that the foods you eat might also affect how you think and feel? Maybe by changing what you eat, you can be happier or smarter!

Picture this: It's the middle of the night and you're lying in bed, wide awake. You wonder if a snack will help you sleep. If you choose right, you might drift off to dreamland. But eat the wrong snack, and you'll still be awake when the birds begin to sing. What will it be? Some foods help people feel relaxed and sleepy: cereals, crackers, potatoes, or pasta, for example. But who wants spaghetti in the middle of the night? How about a cup of warm milk? For many people, that's just the right thing for relaxation.

How about this: It's one of those awful days when everything seems to go wrong for you. What foods will make you feel better? Super-sweet snacks, such as candy or soda, can give you a quick lift. But beware: Those sweets will let you down with a crash in a short while. Instead, try a handful of Brazil nuts, a glass of milk, or a spinach salad. All these foods contain nutrients that seem to lift spirits and help fight the blues.

But why do certain foods affect our moods? The answer is complex and has to do with certain chemicals called neurotransmitters. Neurotransmitters carry messages to and from our brains. Neurotransmitters do more than carry messages. They also produce some of our moods, such as happiness or relaxation. Many neurotransmitters are built from the foods we eat. If you don't eat enough of a certain food, your brain might not be able to make enough of the neurotransmitter that helps you feel energetic. As a result, you might feel sleepy instead of awake.

So the next time you feel sad because you had a fight with your best friend, try a glass of milk and a handful of Brazil nuts instead of that soda. You might be surprised at how much better you feel.

Brynie, Faith Hickman. "Can Milk Make You Happy?" *Appleseeds*, Nov. 2008. *Cricket Media*, Carus Publishing Company.

Name:

Handout 27C:
Author's Point and Reasons

Directions: Use the chart below to organize the points and reasons in "Can Milk Make You Happy?" Use the questions to help you complete each row.

Point: What does the author want you to believe or think after reading this text?

Reasons:

What's the first reason the author gives for believing her point?

What's the second reason the author gives for believing her point?

What's the third reason the author gives for believing her point?

Name: _____

Handout 28A: Word Parts

Directions:

1. Box or circle the prefix or suffix.
2. Use the meaning of the word part and the root word to create a definition for the word.
3. Choose at least five words to write the definition or sketch a picture that represents its meaning.

quickly	harmful
indigestible	mouthful
unwanted	undigested
nonfood	replanted
impossible	delightful
slowly	unused

Name:

Handout 29A: End-of-Module Task Evidence Organizer

Directions: Use this Evidence Organizer to record evidence to help you choose a nutritious meal in preparation for the End-of-Module Task.

PLATE 1		
FOOD	REASON	EVIDENCE

PLATE 2		
FOOD	REASON	EVIDENCE

Name: _____

Handout 32A: Opinion Writing Checklist

Directions: Circle ☺ Yes or ☹ Not Yet to answer each prompt. Then, set a writing goal.

Comprehension	Self	Peer	Teacher
I understand how to make good food choices.	☺ ☹ Yes Not Yet	☺ ☹ Yes Not Yet	☺ ☹ Yes Not Yet
Structure	**Self**	**Peer**	**Teacher**
I respond to all parts of the prompt.	☺ ☹ Yes Not Yet	☺ ☹ Yes Not Yet	☺ ☹ Yes Not Yet
I introduce the topic I am writing about.	☺ ☹ Yes Not Yet	☺ ☹ Yes Not Yet	☺ ☹ Yes Not Yet
I write an opinion statement.	☺ ☹ Yes Not Yet	☺ ☹ Yes Not Yet	☺ ☹ Yes Not Yet
I write two or more reasons to support my opinion statement.	☺ ☹ Yes Not Yet	☺ ☹ Yes Not Yet	☺ ☹ Yes Not Yet

I write one or more pieces of evidence about the reasons.	🙂 😐 Yes Not Yet	🙂 😐 Yes Not Yet	🙂 😐 Yes Not Yet
I write a conclusion that restates or repeats the opinion.	🙂 😐 Yes Not Yet	🙂 😐 Yes Not Yet	🙂 😐 Yes Not Yet
Development			
I use linking works to make connections between sentences.	🙂 😐 Yes Not Yet	🙂 😐 Yes Not Yet	🙂 😐 Yes Not Yet
Conventions			
I use my best spelling. **A B C**	🙂 😐 Yes Not Yet	🙂 😐 Yes Not Yet	🙂 😐 Yes Not Yet
I use end punctuation. **. ? !**	🙂 😐 Yes Not Yet	🙂 😐 Yes Not Yet	🙂 😐 Yes Not Yet
I write complete sentences that have subjects and verbs.	🙂 😐 Yes Not Yet	🙂 😐 Yes Not Yet	🙂 😐 Yes Not Yet
Total number of 🙂 :			

Name:

My writing goal is _____

_____

_____

Teacher Feedback

Name: _____

Handout 32B:
Socratic Seminar Self-Reflection

Directions: Use one of the letters below to describe how often you performed each action during the Socratic Seminar. Then, during the Deep Dive, complete the reflection questions below.

<u>A</u> = I always did that.

<u>S</u> = I sometimes did that.

<u>N</u> = I'll do that next time.

Expectation	Evaluation (A, S, N)
I spoke on topic.	
I listened to appreciate.	
I looked at the speaker.	

I recounted my experience of a good eating choice, including sharing how it made me feel.	
Expectation	**Evaluation (A, S, N)**
I spoke only when no one else was speaking.	
I used kind words.	
I varied inflection when speaking.	

Reflection questions:

1. In preparation for today's lesson, you tried a new food.

   a. What new food did you try? _____

   b. Where did you try it? _____

   c. Who were you with? _____

Name:

2. Look back to your answers for question 1. Use this information to complete the following sentence:

When I tried eating _____ , I was _____ with

_____ . I was speaking _____ because

_____

3. Think about today's Socratic Seminar. Circle whether you spoke formally or informally.

      formally   informally

4. Support the answer you circled. Why do you think you spoke that way?

_____

_____

_____

G2 > M4 > WIT & WISDOM®

Volume of Reading Reflection Questions

Good Eating, Grade 2, Module 4

Student Name: _____

Text: _____

Author: _____

Topic: _____

Genre/type of book: _____

Share your knowledge by responding to the questions below.

Informational Texts

1. **Wonder:** After looking at and reading the cover of this book, what do you notice? What do you wonder?

2. **Organize:** What are the key ideas and details in this book? Verbally recount the key ideas in the book. Be sure to use complete sentences as you speak.

3. **Reveal:** How do the text features in this book help you to find information quickly? Choose one text feature and explain how it helped you find quick information. Remember that some examples of text features are captions, bold print, subheadings, glossaries, and indexes.

4. **Distill:** What big idea did the author want you to take away from reading this book? Find the page or line that most strongly communicates that big idea. Was the author wanting to answer a question, explain something, or describe something?

5. **Know:** What important information did you learn from reading this book? How did the author connect one piece of important information to another piece of important information? Draw a picture to illustrate the connection.

6. **Vocabulary:** Create a list with three important "things" in this text. Tell how each thing is used.

Literary

1. **Wonder:** What details do you notice about the cover that give you clues to what this story will be about? What questions do you have about the details you noticed?

2. **Organize:** What's happening in the text? Retell the story to a friend using complete sentences.

3. **Reveal:** Describe how the illustrator adds to the story in this book. Tell one way the illustrations add to the characters, the setting, and the plot (the beginning, middle, and end in the story.)

4. **Distill:** What lesson can you learn from this book? Draw a picture to show how you might apply the lesson learned.

5. **Know:** How does this story add to what you have learned about "good eating" from other stories or books? Have you learned more about "good eating" from stories or informational texts? Why?

6. **Vocabulary:** Choose three words from the story that describe food in this text. Write a sentence using the three words.

WIT & WISDOM FAMILY TIP SHEET

WHAT IS MY GRADE 2 STUDENT LEARNING IN MODULE 4?

Wit & Wisdom is our English curriculum. It builds knowledge of key topics in history, science, and literature through the study of excellent texts. By reading and responding to stories and nonfiction texts, we will build knowledge of the following topics:

Module 1: A Season of Change

Module 2: The American West

Module 3: Civil Rights Heroes

Module 4: Good Eating

In Module 4, *Good Eating*, we will study the digestive system and the importance of healthy food choices. By analyzing texts and art, students answer the question: *How does food nourish us?*

OUR CLASS WILL READ THESE BOOKS

Picture Books (Informational)

- *The Digestive System*, Christine Taylor-Butler
- *The Digestive System*, Jennifer Prior
- *Good Enough to Eat*, Lizzy Rockwell
- *The Vegetables We Eat*, Gail Gibbons

Picture Books (Literary)

- *Bone Button Borscht*, Aubrey Davis
- *Stone Soup*, Marcia Brown

OUR CLASS WILL EXAMINE THESE PAINTINGS:

- *The Beaneater*, Annibale Carracci
- *Cakes*, Wayne Thiebaud
- *Two Cheeseburgers, with Everything (Dual Hamburgers)*, Claes Oldenburg

© Great Minds PBC

OUR CLASS WILL READ THESE ARTICLES:

- "Can Milk Make You Happy?" Faith Hickman Brynie
- "Debate! Should Sugary Drinks Be Taxed?" TIME for Kids

OUR CLASS WILL WATCH THESE VIDEOS:

- "Food and Family," Nadine Burke
- "Try Something New," Jamie Oliver
- "Planting Seeds: The White House Garden and a Brooklyn School Farm"
- "Fruit Veggie Swag"

OUR CLASS WILL VISIT THIS WEBSITE:

- "Eating Your A, B, C's...", *Kids Discover*

OUR CLASS WILL ASK THESE QUESTIONS:

- How can food nourish my body?
- How can food nourish a community?
- Where does nourishing food come from?
- How can I choose nourishing foods?

QUESTIONS TO ASK AT HOME:

As you read with your Grade 2 student, ask:
- How does this text build your knowledge of good eating? Share what you know about good eating.

BOOKS TO READ AT HOME:

- *Strega Nona*, Tomie dePaola
- "A Moose Boosh: A Few Choice Words About Food," Eric-Shabazz Larkin
- *The Seven Silly Eaters*, Mary Ann Hoberman
- *Thunder Cake*, Patricia Polacco
- *Too Many Tamales*, Gary Soto
- *Sopa de Frijoles: Bean Soup**, Jorge Argueta
- *Farmer Will Allen and the Growing Table*, Jacqueline Briggs Martin

- *Your Digestive System*, Rebecca L. Johnson
- *Granny Torrelli Makes Soup*, Sharon Creech
- *The Quest to Digest*, Mary K. Corcoran
- *How Did That Get in My Lunchbox? The Story of Food*, Chris Butterworth
- *Before We Eat: From Farm to Table*, Pat Brisson

*This text is in both English and Spanish.

IDEAS FOR TALKING ABOUT GOOD EATING:

Visit the library together. Ask the librarian to recommend a book on nutrition, or select one of the titles in the list above. Read the text with your Grade 2 student and ask:

- What do you notice and wonder about the foods in this book?
- Would these foods nourish your body? Why or why not?

CREDITS

Great Minds® has made every effort to obtain permission for the reprinting of all copyrighted material. If any owner of copyrighted material is not acknowledged herein, please contact Great Minds® for proper acknowledgment in all future editions and reprints of this module.

- All material from the *Common Core State Standards for English Language Arts & Literacy in History/Social Studies, Science, and Technical Subjects* © Copyright 2010 National Governors Association Center for Best Practices and Council of Chief State School Officers. All rights reserved.

- All images are used under license from Shutterstock.com unless otherwise noted.

- Handout 27B: "Can Milk Make You Happy?" by Faith Hickman Brynie from *Let's Eat*, Appleseeds November 2008. Text copyright © 2008 by Carus Publishing Company. Reprinted by permission of Cricket Media. All Cricket Media material is copyrighted by Carus Publishing d/b/a Cricket Media, and/or various authors and illustrators. Any commercial use or distribution of material without permission is strictly prohibited. Please visit (**http://www.cricketmedia.com/info/licensing2**) for licensing and (**http://www.cricketmedia.com**) for subscriptions.

- For updated credit information, please visit **http://witeng.link/credits**.

ACKNOWLEDGMENTS

Great Minds® Staff

The following writers, editors, reviewers, and support staff contributed to the development of this curriculum.

Karen Aleo, Elizabeth Bailey, Ashley Bessicks, Sarah Brenner, Ann Brigham, Catherine Cafferty, Sheila Byrd-Carmichael, Lauren Chapalee, Emily Climer, Rebecca Cohen, Elaine Collins, Julia Dantchev, Beverly Davis, Shana Dinner de Vaca, Kristy Ellis, Moira Clarkin Evans, Marty Gephart, Mamie Goodson, Nora Graham, Lindsay Griffith, Lorraine Griffith, Christina Gonzalez, Emily Gula, Brenna Haffner, Joanna Hawkins, Elizabeth Haydel, Sarah Henchey, Trish Huerster, Ashley Hymel, Carol Jago, Mica Jochim, Jennifer Johnson, Mason Judy, Sara Judy, Lior Klirs, Shelly Knupp, Liana Krissoff, Sarah Kushner, Suzanne Lauchaire, Diana Leddy, David Liben, Farren Liben, Brittany Lowe, Whitney Lyle, Stephanie Kane-Mainier, Liz Manolis, Jennifer Marin, Audrey Mastroleo, Maya Marquez, Susannah Maynard, Cathy McGath, Emily McKean, Andrea Minich, Rebecca Moore, Lynne Munson, Carol Paiva, Michelle Palmieri, Tricia Parker, Marya Myers Parr, Meredith Phillips, Eden Plantz, Shilpa Raman, Rachel Rooney, Jennifer Ruppel, Julie Sawyer-Wood, Nicole Shivers, Danielle Shylit, Rachel Stack, Amelia Swabb, Vicki Taylor, Melissa Thomson, Lindsay Tomlinson, Tsianina Tovar, Sarah Turnage, Melissa Vail, Keenan Walsh, Michelle Warner, Julia Wasson, Katie Waters, Sarah Webb, Lynn Welch, Yvonne Guerrero Welch, Amy Wierzbicki, Margaret Wilson, Sarah Woodard, Lynn Woods, and Rachel Zindler.

Colleagues and Contributors

We are grateful for the many educators, writers, and subject-matter experts who made this program possible.

David Abel, Robin Agurkis, Sarah Ambrose, Rebeca Barroso, Julianne Barto, Amy Benjamin, Andrew Biemiller, Charlotte Boucher, Adam Cardais, Eric Carey, Jessica Carloni, Dawn Cavalieri, Janine Cody, Tequila Cornelious, David Cummings, Matt Davis, Thomas Easterling, Jeanette Edelstein, Sandra Engleman, Charles Fischer, Kath Gibbs, Natalie Goldstein, Laurie Gonsoulin, Dennis Hamel, Kristen Hayes, Steve Hettleman, Cara Hoppe, Libby Howard, Gail Kearns, Lisa King, Sarah Kopec, Andrew Krepp, Shannon Last, Ted MacInnis, Christina Martire, Alisha McCarthy, Cindy Medici, Brian Methe, Ivonne Mercado, Patricia Mickelberry, Jane Miller, Cathy Newton, Turi Nilsson, Julie Norris, Tara O'Hare, Galemarie Ola, Tamara Otto, Christine Palmtag, Dave Powers, Jeff Robinson, Karen Rollhauser, Tonya Romayne, Emmet Rosenfeld, Mike Russoniello, Deborah Samley, Casey Schultz, Renee Simpson, Rebecca Sklepovich, Kim Taylor.

Early Adopters

The following early adopters provided invaluable insight and guidance for Wit & Wisdom:

- Bourbonnais School District 53 • Bourbonnais, IL
- Coney Island Prep Middle School • Brooklyn, NY
- Gate City Charter School for the Arts • Merrimack, NH
- Hebrew Academy for Special Children • Brooklyn, NY
- Paris Independent Schools • Paris, KY
- Saydel Community School District • Saydel, IA
- Strive Collegiate Academy • Nashville, TN
- Valiente College Preparatory Charter School • South Gate, CA
- Voyageur Academy • Detroit, MI

Design Direction provided by Alton Creative, Inc.

Project management support, production design and copyediting services provided by ScribeConcepts.com

Copyediting services provided by Fine Lines Editing

Product management support provided by Sandhill Consulting